On the Farm

Words by Eugene Booth
Pictures by Derek Collard

RAINTREE CHILDRENS BOOKS
Milwaukee • Toronto • Melbourne • London

Library of Congress Number: 77-7965

1 2 3 4 5 6 7 8 9 0 81 80 79 78 77

Printed and bound in the United States of America.

Library of Congress Cataloging in Publication Data

Booth, Eugene, 1940 —
    On the farm.

    (A Raintree spotlight book)
    SUMMARY: Questions encourage the reader to look at,
think about, and describe scenes from a farm.
    [1. Farm] I. Collard, Derek. II. Title.
PZ7.B6467On [E] 77-7965
ISBN 0-8393-0113-8 lib. bdg.

On the Farm

Look at the farmyard.
How many kinds of animals do you see?
How does a farmyard sound?

What are all the people doing on
the farm? What do you think is going
to happen to them?

Is this what you thought would happen?
What happened to the woman with the
eggs? Where are the pigs running?

What happened to the men carrying
apples? Why did the ladder fall?
What else could happen?

One bull in the field, two goats in the barn, three pigs and four ducks— they are all on the farm.

How many white horses do you see?
How many brown and spotted ones?
Would you like to go riding?

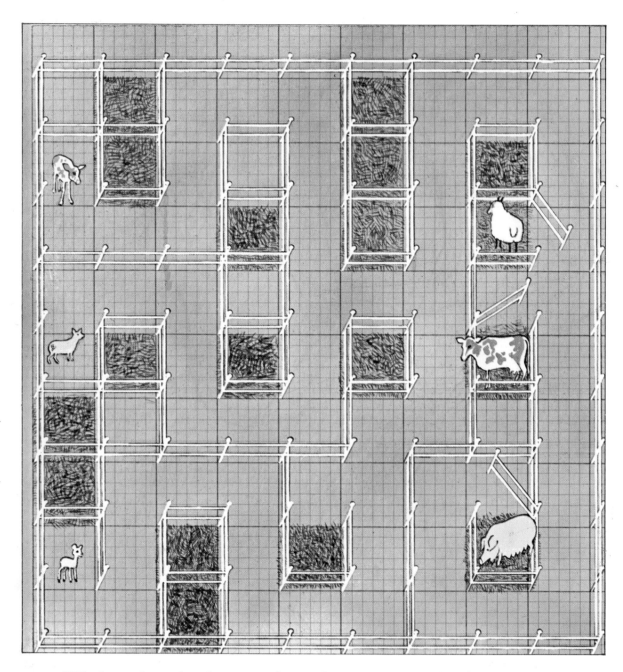

Help the baby animals get to their
mothers. Trace a path with your finger
for each one.

How many big bulls are there?
How many little ones? How many in all?
How many goats and horses?

Here is a market at night.
What are the people doing?
How many people are carrying things?
What do you think is in each box?

What kinds of fruits and vegetables
do you see?

How many cows can you find in this
picture? Some are hard to find.
Look carefully.

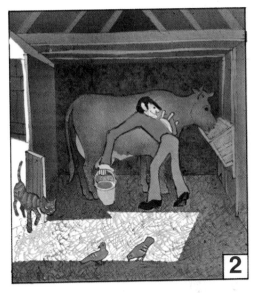

Can you tell a story about these pictures?
What is the man doing? Will the cat
catch the bird?

Is this what you thought would happen?
Did the cat get what it wanted?
What could happen next?

Look at the shapes at the bottom of the page. How many of the shapes can you find in the picture?

Here are machines that you see
on a farm. Can you name them all?
Do you know what they do?

Help put the machines into the field.
Match each one with the right shape.

There are all kinds of things wrong
in this picture.

How many mistakes can you find?
Look carefully.